11:11

ANASTASIYA
SUKHENKO

11:11

Storytelling House

To:

my mom who has been my rock.

My family in Ukraine who has inspired so much strength.

Kiana, who has sat in the trenches with me
and shown me soulmates do exist.

Victor, for your creative wisdom.

Sarah, for embracing all of my weirdness.

Richard, for encouraging me to be brave.

Tori, for never doubting me.

Autumn, for your endless love.

Ashley, for your poetic heart.

And to my writing buddy and editor, Casey for reading my
worst poems and pretending to like them.

I love you all.

First Printing, 2022

CONTENTS

1. LOVE

CONTENTS

CONTENTS

Introduction

I never thought I would pull together a collection of words, let alone under the guise of poetry. But here it is, and I couldn't be more excited or terrified.

I struggled the most with thinking of a theme because I had written about love, friendship, stars, existence, loss, and every other nuance of life that made me stop what I was doing, dive into my Notes app, and scramble to form something cohesive from my thoughts.

In the end, I never really found a theme. Instead, I found a title that seemed to embody the chapter of my life while I was more seriously piecing this book together.

I had just moved from my home state, Florida, to another sunny state, California. And for some reason, I continued to see the numbers 111 and 11:11 every day. I found myself clinging to these numbers like a sign from the universe that I was on the right path.

I was trying to find certainty in my choices, just as I try to find meaning in my life through writing.

Were these numbers significant? I don't know. But I've given them purpose with this book.

I've learned there's nothing quite like the bond between humanity and the unknown. Nothing like the ecstasy it brings when you meet a new lover. Or like the gut punch when you fall in love. Nothing like the curiosity of childhood as you grasp at a new world. Or like losing control of the world around you as you try to make sense of it.

There is nothing more beautiful, chaotic, and scary than navigating life.

This book, I suppose, is about just that. It's about the unknown. It's about everything I've learned and not learned, but have tried my best to understand.

This is my experience put to paper.

This is for you, me, and everyone who feels lost, or is losing their mind but is trying their best.

Anastasiya

LOVE

regardless of if we make it to winter, this will be a spectacle.

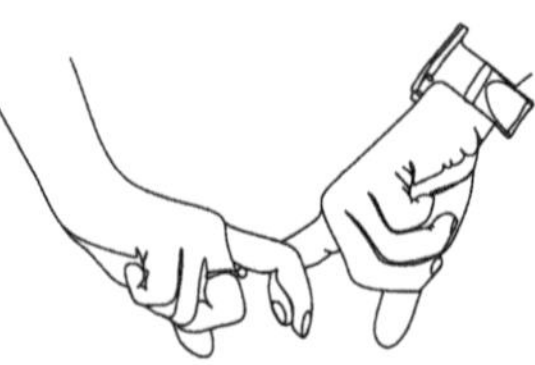

summer air

there is something about summer air that makes you want to fall in love. the breeze. the heat. the pockets of freedom. something so innocent about the start of June. something so untamed about the slow-burn afternoons. something so sweetly aching about the nights as you fall into someone new...

experiment

it was the first time i had listened to my body instead of my mind.
we were not magnets
pulled by some strange, singular gravity
that solely the two of us were obliged to.
nor was it instant,
like lightning,
but there was thunder.
the delayed kind that makes you wonder,
wait.
count the seconds of silence,
anticipation writhing,
as to whether
it'll make a sound.
a buzzing in the fibers of my skin:
the quick moving of electrons
finding their place with you by my side.
you pulled away
to do the work you were obliged to,
and i was left analyzing these strange chemicals in my body
(make me do even stranger things)
that only emote for you.
this was an experiment,
and i was both the test subject and the researcher.
would a brush of your hand redden my cheeks?
from a distance,
your eyes fixed on me,
my thoughts became molten
oozing down my spine.
bear with me

as i study this
obsessively in the night.

in flux

sage the room!
there's a new lover

their scent will stay with you
and June will fight to last the whole year

spoiler —
June will lose

not even fantasy-drenched nights
and the primal tether in your body are stronger than

the merciless sever: time

the psychic said:
to move on, empty the lavender
in your pockets

empty your heart

okay, i said. and i did —
scattered the remains of something once perfect
to later become an ancient artifact of the moonlight-rush

that enters your bloodstream, maybe once
every lifetime
if you're lucky

but i kept the midnight
when it rained that one night in LA
and i heard for the first time, tucked into your chest,

11:11

the clock confess:
you took a risk stepping into the opening,
to see all that is finite rush towards you. to know

there is an end from the very beginning and know
these are things you cannot change.

lover's hex

throw in the magic charms

this is madness, and i can't wait

to discover you

to discover how we poison ourselves for pleasure

and ask why our bodies are blue

it must look like gibberish

to anyone who is not us

it must look like falling

to me and not you

it must be thirty-six seconds i've known you

supernatural

my favorite conversations are the ones held through our eyes. the mystery of what is unsaid keeps me locked in with you. but even if you were to say, “i love you,” it would not encompass the moment you looked at me and turned away, smiling into your pillow. it would not say what was unsaid: that whatever flows between us is so fragile, and so remarkable. that, this, is a synapse. that it’ll go away. that maybe love is a choice, but the current between us — that is magic — and for a moment, we held it.

mania

does it drive you crazy? *the moment their hand brushed over yours and instinct left you like your breath.*

do you think about it all the time? *the euphoria that vanished just as quickly as it came.*

will you do anything for more? *bruise your knees and lose your mind. let your heart become your guide.*

let them become your god.

surrender

i open my mouth wider
for you to trace the words *you're mine*

my submission is a whisper
but hedonism *listens* and *acts* even in silence

my days are no longer days
my hours are no longer hours
my state is in the gloaming; the blurring ephemeral
where boundaries are tempted and touched
and misunderstood

shivered into surrender, i linger
and you flicker this is our language
and i don't have to explain

two bodies under pale light

do the moths look at us
like we look at two stars colliding?

i listen to you breathe in
and out

there are no words between us
in these hours

there could be no words
ever again

and it wouldn't change
that your blue
has mixed with mine

and i can't see blue
without you
anymore

supermoon

i've expanded myself
for you

into the pearly abyss

of old and new
teeth scars
that crater my body

it's a supermoon kinda love kinda extreme
to sit so close to you
under this light
and let you see all my wounds

i guess you caught me on a rare day

i guess we're all spinning
and for whatever reason

i was always moving toward you

candy days repeating

melted hard candy
to my ears.
fill my head,
so sweet (too sweet
to be good).
harden over my brain
only to crack
from a head tap
at the end of the day.
i'll wake up
ready to choose sugar
over air
again.

in Paris

my head hits the pillow
as yours rises

i cannot take in this sight

my veins cannot drink its wine
my heart cannot swoon for dazzling lights

not since my lungs have carried over
to the other side of the world

your moonwater

running with you

how different it is to like someone that you worry you could disappoint. unlike the others that i daydreamed about, deliberating what burning impulse they would direct at me as i detailed some small nothing about myself. no, it's entirely different to like someone and wonder if you'll stay good enough for them. of course, this is only the beginning. i haven't even crossed the line of falling in love. but by then, i'll be running alongside them, musing which of us is trying to keep up. and after that, i'll be in love. i'll learn that all this time it was both of us, not only in competition with one another, but in support.

moment.

your lips, my eyes
try to think of anything more

clean, crisp bedsheets wrap around us
i stare at you long enough to trust you

at least in this moment,

i believe in God
i believe no bomb will be dropped
and that everyone in the world is experiencing something perfect

at least in this moment.

your hands, my thighs
who wanted who first?

this view
painted by the pupils of your eyes

i ignore the looming thought of impermanence

(i think, lavender will be my last memory of you).

religious

i once met a man who told me he was not religious. but every morning and every night, he would speak with a girl he had never met. in his dreams, he would call to her. in his waking day, he would look for signs of her. he told me he was not religious, but i have never seen greater devotion than from a man with a bleeding heart lick salt from another's wound.

card tricks

you placed The Lovers gently
on the top of my palm.
their heads directly above my wrist
and their feet aimed at my fingertips.
enlivened by your use of black magic,
i didn't see the true meaning within
your promise.
i revealed to you mine,
upright and honest: The Fool.
for a moment, i was distracted
by the spark in your eyes — yet another
one of your magic tricks.
i didn't see
the slight of your hand
flip my card and change our fate.

somewhere

in a false forever,
    she lay in his arms
and became someone less
    like herself. less like a sapling,

more like a dense lace of the dark moon

too complex for her to unravel loneliness
and love, and the need for hands that
are not hers.

secrecy is intoxicating,
delicacy behind touch and speech
among lovers — from lovers.

what i do and you don't know won't hurt you.
but it'll hurt me and i'll hold that hurt
to keep loving you.

in the same fashion as fine leather and heavy silk,
she's learned that love is woven from death and made
beautiful after so much pain.

she prefers the ache over the hollow,
    and after she untangles from his arms,
the air presses around her wincing
    over not the loss of him, but the absence

of the woman last night, the woman sprawled over the
first shred of light, the woman who cannot find herself
whole.

obsession

i've found that i can be miserable in almost any city. i've also found that there is no distraction quite as distracting as my obsession for you. sometimes i wonder if i am so mentally ill that my desire for love debilitates me. and now that i've had a glimpse of it, i can do nothing else but think of it. it's a crumb, but one that i will savor and never swallow. not until i am bare bones. and even then, i find myself doubting if i will be willing to swallow it gone.

night is falling

and i'm standing under it. it's hysterical what
we'll put ourselves through for what we can't keep.

the stars whisper: *to hope, to hope.*

the air tastes of honey, and i know you're near.

i drink it in,

lover's venom, poisoning my mind with thoughts
of an end.

the gods are cruel
to give me you.

i've been asleep between the waves for so many years;
not happy, but not suffering.

i don't need the gospel to know the whole story.
i've had love seep into my soul and pain suck me dry.

the sky is swirling with heartbreak.

baby, can you hear it? night is falling

and this is only the beginning.

train wreck

so, yeah, it hurts like a bitch   like darkness
screaming back   i should've known when
we boarded the same train   you would survive the
wreck   because you didn't go into it willing
   to wreck yourself

silly girl   that's what they'll say   but i was
young   never been in love   the warning lights
looked like headlights   and i wanted so badly
to believe   you would save me
from the wreckage   that you would come back
that you couldn't leave this   that what we had
was more than summer

artifice

i spoke with someone on the train
and not about how we each hold our own cataclysms.
we talked about flowers and the price of everything living
and i almost brought up the patterns of me and you
but the breath-stab stopped me.

it's a falsehood to hope if i mouth your name,
i'll cast a kinetic fever and you'll find your lips
parting, thinking of me

but the falsehood is all i have to keep me
from wreckage to my fundamental.

i'm struggling
and if i were to treat every stranger on the train
like a confessional, i'd admit
i've kept the falsehood in my pocket long enough
for it to turn into a deranged coin, murmuring,
luck. toss me to the water. send your last wish.

and when the crises cries out to me
from inside the night, the falsehood becomes
the last pill in the bottle that i safe-keep
on my nightstand under the lamplight

what was the falsehood   lifetimes of me and you

i'll say it anyway

there is no pretty way to say, "i miss you." we are not pretty. our love is not pretty. it is a mess where all the colors spill over each other, and the canvas suffocates under its weight.

but i miss you.

and i'd go back to you over and over again, even as our friends cry out to us in horror. i'd suffer you to keep us, as ugly as we are, because the pain i feel without you is worse than the pain i feel with you.

trapped

i cannot fight this —
like a moth against a hurricane i will die in your storm.
but i succumb to my instinct and fight for survival. i know
it's hollow to try. i've been pulled in by your force.
i'm trapped inside.
your effect spins me round: a dizzying sight, confusion
committed to fright.
all i can do is wait,
and pray,
that i not only come out alive but with my wings
unscathed.
even more hollow
is my hope.

nothing quite like

there is nothing quite like a person who falls in love quickly. they obsess in the night about their new potential lover. it blows their mind that they can find a love like this. it blows their mind that feelings exist like this! and here they are, existing for them. but nothing is quite as destructive as when the love they have for lover goes unwanted, and they ask themselves, *where do i put it all?*

deep end

i tasted your spit and confused it for love
and let your silence speak stories of a hoax.
i realized we both stepped off the deep end,
and not together.

i miss the days when our feet dangled off the edge
and summer was too hot to blacklist winter. i miss
the dreaming of jumping because the dreaming
was the best part. because before then, we
had both dreamt of a winter not so cold, of our
bodies entangled forever.

beggar

non-dreams are really not fun
especially when your knees buckle and
you're forced to take a time-out.

you're asleep
and i'm on a hospital floor,

that's the reality
no matter how hard i bite down.

i'm a beggar. a heartbreak fool. a child showing their painting
to no one who cares.
a beggar. a heartbreak fool. a —

girl, strumming her heart
softly
as if it were apple-skin.
strumming to the deepest echo of the night,
throwing in her last penny, begging. waiting.
her heart pried open for the morning to unfold —
the wonderwork.
bring me the supernatural
that brings me to your eyes. bring me all that
i promised you. bring me
you.

pain

the worst part about pain is that no one will feel it for you. you have to feel it all for yourself: every degree, every wave, every storm without warning. and those who can't brace it cling to other people — the way you'd cling to a life raft if you believed you couldn't swim. because the only thing worse than the pain, is to bear it alone.

maybe

i want to write to you, but what does that say about me? maybe i need clarity to see what it means. maybe i have so much love that i don't always know where it should go. maybe you don't deserve me, but maybe i just want to have fun too. maybe i want to kiss you a few more times before hearts break a little more. maybe i'm not ready to give up the feeling you give me. maybe you're bad for me and i'm good for you.

maybe,

it's time i let go.

people

there are going to be people you meet who leave your head dizzy. people who teach you about currents and electricity by a mere stroke of their hand. you will discover a different shade of red unique to your face and feel summer beneath your skin. you will think this is love, the highest form of ecstasy. you will chase that feeling and the person who gave it to you, unconvinced that you will find it again from somebody else.

until the day you do.

and maybe you will experience this a handful of more times. it'll feel new every time. it'll be hard every time. you will survive every time.

distance

my eyes will not look ahead.
they will look away,
where it's safe. where you're there,
speaking the right words,
standing by my side.
until, one day,
this place empties.
i'll fill it with all my favorite flowers,
oceans, mountains, valleys —
every part of myself.
and it'll be so full
that i'll forget about
your footprints
buried in the sand.
and the touch of your hands
once buried in my hair.

obsession is not love

i've found
after this delusion,
fully lived in,
a sense of peace
in our goodbye.

mania has fallen dormant;
dulled its nails.
i can sleep knowing
that knowing you
is enough.

my film

i play it over in my mind — your hips pressed into mine, standing in the kitchen, the music playing. i'm glad this is a part of my film, that our love was set in a burning city and the kitchen light made everything look so soft. i play it over in my mind, even though it's over now. i know we've moved on. i know our love is a smaller vessel compared to the bigger vessels, but i wouldn't have missed it for the world. without you, without our little love, my film would have never been complete.

DARK PLACES

to the kids born into their parent's fire,
raised with singed minds,
sold on paper dreams —

how were we ever supposed to survive?

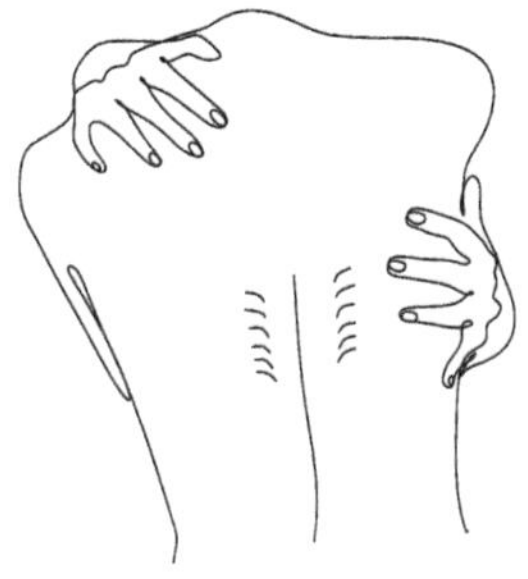

to the house

near the lake that encircles the cul-de-sac;

murky water, snapping
turtles, baby alligators,
stale bread.

you saw and heard it all;

no wall, no door

shielded you.
and sometimes secrets spilled;

bleeding umber walls,
canopied streets,
abutting suburbans.

a bountiful burden;

shattered TV glass,
clandestine candy
hidden in cabinets,
brain bits.

years have passed. each one
baked into birthday cakes;

milestone chocolate,
three-layer depression
funfetti, forgettery
vanilla, lonesome
coconut.

the same water courses through,
and the nosy trees listen
to the new family;

silver and sapphirine
cars, plastic playhouse
and scattered playthings,
patched walls painted
in corrective cream.

perhaps, this family will do better.

haunted

adults are ghosts to children in unhappy homes. they haunt the hallways that are supposed to lead us to greater destinations. they haunt the rooms that are supposed to be our safe place. and just like ghosts, they never age, and they never die. no matter how many years pass, how old the child gets, whether they have children themselves — if their home was unhappy, they will leave with a haunted heart.

modern horror story

i'll tell you a modern horror story: the hero took off the cape, tied it around their neck, and stepped off. the villain saw an opportunity, so they never told anyone the hero had died long, long ago. *let them believe they can be saved. let them never learn to save themselves.*

inner child

there is a child in all of us running the show. when our anger takes hold, or the loneliness is too much to bear. when love becomes terrifying or a means of an escape. there is a child in all of us who bore the most of our pain. the child who felt the blade twist in their heart and knew their childhood had ended. this is the child who needed the most protection. the child who needed the most love. remember to be kind to yourself, love yourself, and never abandon who you are. then one day, the child will trust you enough to let go of the reins.

an old friend

i had a dream about an old friend,
a dead friend.
he was more than that
a hero, a mentor, a father.
but i've grown older,
he's aged no more;
immortalized in a memory
that i was too afraid to surface
into the light
like a ship
buried in the deep, unlit sea.
but i've grown older.
he's grown not at all.
and now his memory has crumbled,
like the ship brought to light;
impossible to repair
for everything was already destroyed.
he was only held intact
because he was held in the dark.

void

people will come and go, and there will be some people who exit your life forever. whether they give you a warning or not, there is no amount of preparation to prepare you for the weight of absence. it's heavier than any feeling. it's the broken promise of a person — of a life that could've been shared with yours. to lose someone, when that someone felt permanent, is to learn that Hell is not fire. it is an open void containing all the burden of all our unmet desires.

leech

i'll tell you this much / the wormhole darkness
in my chest is not a hypothetical

i feel the fingers of my father / wrap around my heart
like it never belonged to me

and i think / there is no escape
from that place

from that hell / from chlorine-filled lungs
and leeches carrying my birthday cake

i want to scream / from the ocean floor
so i can ache without causing a scene

i'm an adult now / i know / i know /
and i promise / i'm trying really hard

from becoming a leech myself /
and i really hope when i die / you'll say

goodnight / sweetling /
you were so / so loved

i will see you in the brighter morning /
and this time / it will not be so hard

to learn

you can't cure someone's childhood. you can't scrape the abuse — their pain. you can't pull out the rot in their heart without pulling out their whole heart. you can't tell them to grow up. not when they never learned how. but you can stop the rot from spreading. you can end the abuse. break the wheel. you can hold their hand through their darkest days. you can stay. you can teach them if they've never learned what it means to be cared for. you can show them what it means to love.

Florida fever dream

at the center of lakes, thunderous rainstorms,
and billboards promoting events that sell death
packaged in a metal boomerang,
is a young girl with pigtails running through fertilized fields.

she feeds stale bread to the lurking alligators
behind her house.
the house that is surrounded by both palm
and coniferous trees.
she has dreams of alligators biting at her feet. but forgets
to heed
the person sleeping below them.
in the summer, the power goes out
and candles decorate every room.
she learns what a proper heart looks like in the dark.
the air is wet, hot; smothering like an unwanted kiss.
the bugs bounce around her; it's their party.
but she is the disco ball.

the times of days are painted in different colors of light:
it's 6 AM,
the world is grey and pink.
12 PM
is gold-tinted green.
white-hot extends from 1 to 3.
orange creeps behind blue until 5:30.
and all the colors fight for the big show around 7.
it's like a painting,
painted with melted Starbursts and watercolor.
maybe it's a Van Gogh?
or the very moment

that would have inspired the solar sister to The Starry Night.

most of her time is spent driving
from one nowhere to another.
but she enters all the seasons of her mind.
the rainbow reflects the storm and the light.
it couldn't exist without the two.
everyone drives too fast
because everyone drives too slow. it's busywork.
and eventually, she'll end up at the beach
where the sand burns her feet and
the seawater soothes.
the moment will taste salty
but the memory will smell like tangerine
and wild strawberries.

sun addicts

we were raised in the place
where the elders come retire.

it's always summer here
and our minds are always on fire.

we love sunburnt shoulders,
rashes under skin,
and feral frustrations from overthinking.

we burn ourselves
to avoid the void of boredom.

summer break

the lights never go out here.

not during a storm,
not even a recession.
they're fluorescent.
perfect for every boxed product
and scabbed Florida orange.

here, we ride the bikes
too expensive for the streets.
but it's reckless fun
getting kicked out of a store.

we spend our money on candy:
the staple of children
raised with no boundaries.

we run barefoot in the streets
exempt from the bikes we can't afford.
the mosquitoes cling to us,
and we cling to youth.

the summer air is so hot,
our blood is so sweet,
and youth is so free
only once.

lightning

this youth —
what can i compare it to?
like lightning threatening to strike
asphalt cracked
by careless drivers
and too many
who have walked this road before.

dark place

there's a threshold, and i've reached it, for how long
i can blame those who raised me.

i guzzle down nitroglycerin and caffeine
for superpowers (and normalcy) and
start each day the same way i end it:

locking eyes with the umbral of humanity
and stepping past it.

:

DREAMS & OTHER THINGS

the dreamers are the ones
who have lived countless lives.
they dream of more.
they see more.
they want more.
after all, how could this single life
be enough when they
have dreamed infinitely?

it's all one line

the further away i move from
the infinite black of night,
the night before the start of my journey
through gaseous forms of color and light,
i don't move any further at all.

happiness

if you asked me to describe happiness, i would need a kaleidoscope. i would show you: happiness is a constantly changing assortment of people, places, and time. i would tell you, do not chase it. feelings are not meant to be chased or caged. chasing it will drive it further away. caging it will smother it. feelings are meant to come and go. they are meant to be known. then they are meant to be let go.

fear

fear is a balancing act. fear protects you. fear propels you. allow fear to be an ally, and it will kindle the flame inside your heart. allow fear to be an enemy, and it will send waves to drown what inspires.

how do you choose to see the world?

often, i see us treat it as a limited buffet with so little food for too many people — and like savages, we rush to take what we can before it's gone.

but i don't think the world is that finite. i think there is an infinite amount of experience, love, and opportunity. i think that someone else's success is not a stolen opportunity from you. it is an opportunity that you are not meant for.

i believe the world knows what you need and presents it to you when the moment is right. so, when someone does succeed, stand and cheer for them. give them the same love you want to be given to you when your moment comes — because it will.

monster

we spend so much time worrying about things that will never happen to us. more often, it's the things we don't even think of that happen to us. we shouldn't suffer a hundred times over for what we can't control. that's all worrying is: a means of tricking our minds that we're doing something to prevent tragedy from happening. if you can, try not to worry so much. allow for the good and the bad, the beauty and the ugly, and know that the unknown is far often kinder than the monster we make it out to be in our heads.

scale your summons

from the mountain peak,
you've reached
a height once dreamed
and stand quite high
only to see another mountain.

if only the reward
for such a feat
allowed you to step upon clouds,
soft but sturdy —
traverse you to another summit.

no,
our reward,
the greatest one to achieve,
is to realize
you can reach heights once unseen.

daydreaming

everything we dream of
is a call into the void
to be loved a little more.

inside

all of us is a dream meant to be explored. a dream that has its own timeline separate from the one the world convinces you it should be. a dream that reveals itself slowly. a dream that takes its time to come true.

don't rush. trust. the best things in life are not an explosion offering a short-lived moment of excitement. the best things in life are long-lasting, durable. they build upon layers of hard work, pain, and persistence. and holding those layers together are slices of joy, passion, and faith.

Heaven

perhaps, Heaven is a library.
there, we'll uncover all the stories
immortalized in blank pages,
invisible scriptures,
saved only for the beholder
willing to open the books.

a billion years

i never thought too much about the universe
until i watched a cobweb collect the dust
of a room where nothing happened
and i wondered
how much of everything is really
nothing
and how much luck do we really get
to get
something
and how often is that
"something"
the marvel behind two eyes
linked with two other eyes
that scream mystery

and in a billion years
how often will
that

exist

again
on another planet
in another galaxy
during another timeline

how often will two eyes meet
and form histories yet to exist
and wish for nothing more
than violet nights

stars

i will let you in on a secret:

you are among the stars.

you are made of the collision; the kaleidoscopic chaos that formed the constellations we ponder with childlike wonder. you are made of all the things we cherish. so, please, cherish yourself. gaze into your eyes, see your spark and soul harmonize, and know that you are alive. trace the sunspots over your skin and form stories as you would with star myths. experience your thoughts spell your mind so bright and far-reaching like starlight, then collapse into itself with a burst of dynamite. collect the remnants and reinvent. form new thoughts, patterns, and planets. discover yourself bring into existence all that you ever dreamed. then dream again.

bona fide

don't look too closely
or it'll all look like a wasteland.
everything is everywhere and no one needs
to look at you for you to be some ceremonious carbon.

there are bruises on the sidewalk from heavy expectation
and i'm learning from following other footsteps
that a lifespan is a stupor and i'm tired of trying to
squeeze destiny for a kernel of celestial worth.

sometimes, most times, i want playfulness to
feel palpable instead of the mounting manmade
reckoning that haunts every one of my decisions.

we treat this as an investment, and maybe it is,
but it's exhausting when everything needs to aim
for something.

i'm not encouraging throwing up hands and
wreaking havoc, there's a deadness in that that i don't want
to explore. i just want to throw up hands and let the
sunlight caress them, let the atoms in my body yawn
and slug in the luminous kingdom come,

leave the examiner tools behind and know with no
convincing that we were absorbed into light before
night ever came.

TO BE HUMAN

a truly human existence is dancing with insanity. you cannot live fully as a human without having madness take you at least once.

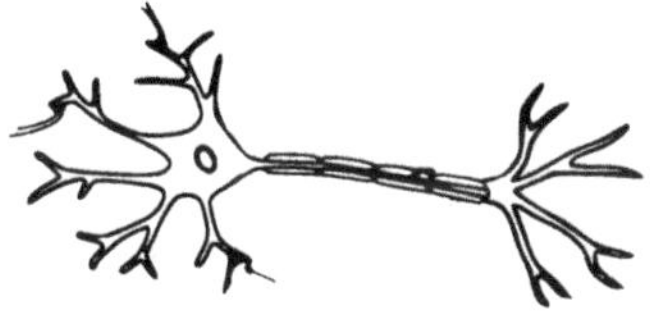

fire and water

i once knew a girl who was born on a full moon. restless in the night, the water in her body overflowed with emotions. and when the sun came, it set her mind aflame. inside her waged an endless battle between two extremes: who she is and who she wishes to be.

how to be a modern-day woman

it's not enough to be young and sweet.
you need to be violently sexy
and your sexy must fit into 1080 pixels, and come from
cold-pressed juices and cigarettes but
you can never be seen drinking milk

you need six side-hustles and at least one of them
must show your tits because that's celebrated now
and capitalized since feminism is capitalized

just don't forget to get a 1420 on your SAT
so people can take you
seriously. oh, and come from a town
no one cares about
so, when you move to a town
everyone cares about,
you'll be cool and new
and your Who Cares town will regard you
like some glittery spectacle,
and the dads back home
will pretend not to watch your OnlyFans

and guess what? God apparently has a gender
— and it's yours!
since sparkly popstar
basically modern-day prophet
told us so,
and she also told us, God has many kinks like
being worshiped and degraded
worshipped and degraded
worshipped being tied up

newly modern way
of lighting a candle

but don't let lover know   you think of them
no less   than 12 hours a day

now that God is a woman   you don't need to nurture
you need praise   from lover   from world
you need to know   that this is the best it's ever been
for us girls

look at us! living in a modern world!

soft-face girls

i think about the soft-face girls
hidden in the underbelly

i think about the faces they wear
and the mirrors they avoid

i think about the sidewalks they stand on
and how many shadows walk over them

i wonder who they turn to
on lonely nights like these

i wonder if the vampires ever think
"enough."

i know their biggest secret is not
what's in their bloodstream or who's in their bed

i know their biggest secret is who they dreamt
of becoming

i know their biggest fear is their opposite; to
meet their potential if potential was served
on a silver platter

i understand now that a long time ago, the
moon's shadow formed a God complex

and all of this went unchecked because
no one good ever goes searching in the dark

and now so many soft-face girls are born
and are given a mask before they are given a name

and this all makes me so sad because i am
a soft-face girl, and yes i have my masks, but i
also know my name

i know a kind of love that isn't a forced hand and
i've felt warmth more than i've felt cold

and i think why why why are some born *here*
and others born *there*

why is the cosmic spit of some existences a
glassy ball of future horrors

why have we pretended to not see that God
wears masks too

that His solar-flare is one,
the one we love,
and underneath it is the moon

blue madonna

a beautiful woman
and alone.
he sees it as a sin.
he would commit acts of sin to make it not so.
with her hand on her cheek, he watches
as the shadows on her face fall into place
and darkness becomes holy. he wants her
like a wound wants a knife.

mutilation

at a certain age, white noise began to sound
like a piercing hymn forewarning some tragic end.

my eardrums bled, so i dug my nails into my skin
thinking i could stop the clock from tipping.

i'm not sure when i decided bleeding
was as necessary as breathing. i just know

the storm had claimed one direction,
and rather than lay on the sand and suck in toxic fumes
happily,

i pulled myself through glass believing
after enough bloodshed i could withstand
rain.

a calloused heart is windless and silent. *eventually*
there is nothing   eventually

there is a rooted need for what is gone.

open tab

the hours when a gentle squeeze of a lime is felt
more often than the gentle squeeze of a hand —

before the birdcage falls inside my head
and the smell of different stories

all pressed into a single room
slowly peel away the night.

those favored, sung about, driven mad for hours
are when histories are made.

and remade.

when you want nothing more
than to let nightfall push down on you.

the hours that caution
feeling so far from death,

as you hold a drink in one hand,
with one foot   inside its doorstep.

conviction

found only in fiction
are the colors we want from life

we'll do anything to see the spectrum

smash our knuckles into our eyes
to form constellations in the black

swallow our pills dry
to discover a different shade of blue

bury ourselves in books
so our graves are painted with untruth

but it's only pretense
to convince ourselves
that what we're experiencing
is new
revolutionary
worthwhile

spiritual error inside a motel bedroom

picture it: *you*, lying in a bed, holding a conversation
for the neurons in your head.
a globetrotter
stretching the realms of your imagination — promising
choreography spinning with serotonin. safe places.
exotic spaces.
stay sane.
so many bright rectangles in your face, no wonder
we believe in superiority — a better elsewhere.
in the other room, two lovers meet in private
while your parents fight over the phone about who grabbed
the knife first.
you propose a submission to delusion or no more
vitamin deficiency.

the truth? everyone is bored and sad
(probably anemic too)
and craving stimulation. you watch a fly circle the bulb.
who is the main character? the fly
smacks against the window.

this is the interim.

you observe your self-imposed
prison. you have become a servant to observation
finding fascination in all things outside
yourself.
even in your head, you observe *you* through
a third-party lens. the character —
a caricature born from jejune influence.
you speak something mundane through dry-lips

and swirl back to your imaginary world.

you don't think too hard about how your place in this world
is in a low-lit room.   your mind is
elsewhere   in a world inside worlds
and in all the possibilities of something compelling
    you landed here
letting the whole of seconds   look away
    as if *you* in this room are not real —
    as if the burden of shaping yourself
into yourself
    into life
        can be abandoned

life on the shore

is a life in between
the girl with eyes made of sapphire-sprinkled jade,
and the girl crafted from ash
slashing the dragons
with a sword forged from blood.

this is the secret to survival:

silver screen kind of dreams
keep the pills and the shadows hidden
in the smoke.

i've learned to keep my feet buried
in the make-believe sand,
and my head turned towards

the horizon.

currency of my soul

is all the trauma
and freakshow drama
that shades my youth
enough to give me the currency
to be like the *greats?*

i'll poison my mind
and take a gun to the walls i've built —
let secrets spill brutality
and flood my eyes —
let saltwater trickle down my throat
and into my lungs.

i'll suffocate myself,
fill my cavities with more salt —
if i am promised
to be
immortalized in books,
sung from the mouths of heroes,
loved by those i will never know,
and know me. know my name.

is it enough to give my sanity?
or do you want my soul too?
the price for greatness in a single life,
and eternal applause from endless others.
the desire for that sound to ring forever
in the pitch-black —

and sound like music,
to pull me through,

to the other side.

to start again.
to give my soul,
and wish

to be *known.* to be *great.*

to be.

nostalgia whispers, as destiny calls

both a mysterious lover
to sneak in through the back door
and leave without a goodnight's kiss.

i collapse into bed
and my compass points back to a time
i once held with dread. asleep,
i dreamt of sanguine fullness, a time that was
not this.

what will i look like?   *present, beaming.*
what will i feel?   *happy, equipped.*

i did not imagine with prophetic brilliance
i would reminisce slow-flowing years brimming
with shapeless worries.

i did not know with confidence
that i would be okay. through doubt i threaded
the certainty of now. and i question, would i have
been *okay* either way?

i deliberate and come to the conclusion:
the brain ravages
and the soul yearns. i do not appreciate
what is already here.

it is sweet to miss,
like honey dripping from a comb of memories.

it is sweet to wish, like cherry soda bubbling over

from expectation.

and what you once found so dreadful
you now find so good.

it takes work to find the middle satisfaction
of the two —
to not have sweet crystalline coating my tongue or
coursing my veins,
to not feel glutted from destiny
or crave so much from nostalgia.

to one day breathe in so deeply
and have nothing live inside me but this air.

i can feel it now, as i'm writing this,
evanescent presence placing itself in my hands
and passing.

truthkeeper

the body does not betray itself, the mind does. there is nothing more honest than the stiffness of bones, a racing heart, or the cold chills down your back — because the body knows what the mind is not willing to admit.

the body will keep the truths the mind fights to forget.

memory:

a beast and a source of light. it can be
both. like a shapeshifter.

i sometimes feel, after many years, how much
memory eats away at my body. it loves my hips,
that is why they are hollow.

sometimes my body tries to tell me
all the ways i've become empty,
but memory is so strong and persuasive with its
words and visuals. i listen to the wrong things.

my mouth has become a locket
for all the things i tell
and never say
for all the things i swallow
and spit back up.

my eyes bite harder than my teeth, tearing at my
skin *be better* memory reminds me.
memory tears the hardest, it swallows the most

and yet,

memory is what fills me
when it's not eating away.

it shines, even at the precise.
it safe keeps token moments
and polishes them so they gleam with time.

it is

the last source of light
before i shut my eyes
for the final time.

ambition

like a blackening tooth, feeling decay
before death has come, and licking compulsively
to remind yourself you're working your way
to perfect teeth.

sucks you can't smile. but someday.
right? someday you'll start the day with white
and end the day knowing you blinded so many.

that's the dream.
right?

i heard the other day the suit-people say:
the rot has gotten to their brains. it's too late for them.

meaning for us.

meaning i saw on the news
ripples in the mud-sludge flooding the cities.
no one seems to care long enough, and we go back
to dreaming rotten dreams about perfect teeth.

it's not that we're moonblind, it's that we tremble
in the night when we feel another ripple. we want
to forget the news so we can forget the shame. we
want white teeth and no stains. we *want and want*
and want to be blinded by the end of who we are.

bitter

the days protract from pain,
and i peel the lemon anyway.

there is a whole history of misery,
    and what was sharp
    becomes intimate.

my fingers gently skin the bitter;
there is something meditative about
moving without expectation. pain is quiet that way.

like a superpower, i don't know when it will end
and i go on living.

but how long?
how long can i endure
lemon juice in my blood?

silver lining

when all the hurt has hurt
and it comes claws up,
i make a home in its catacombs.

i want to stay nestled in sheets
with only my shaking body. i want to
stay starved so i have moments
of hunger. i want silence to linger
so i can pretend time has stopped.

i want to stay selfish in my sadness: the only
silver lining i can find.

equals

you could say it's skin that makes us equal. or bones. the romantics would venture it's love. the scientists would argue it's a conscious. but to have either, to have any, is to ultimately have pain. to exist is to suffer and survive. that is the narrative of every one of our stories. that is what makes us equal.

rosy

there will be times when you think your life is nothing. and you'll curl up and wait for the emptiness to pass. these will be hard times. these will be times when the psyche abandons itself. these will be times when you question what the "right" decision is. but know that what you believe to be right will change as you age — and with age, even the hardest times will be but an anecdote. find comfort in knowing that everything you look back on will look rosier the farther you grow away from it. in every moment that feels hard, know it will soften with time.

daydrunk

in the Pacific Palisades where time is affluent and stored in tiny seashells, i think of how you've never been this beautiful, and i wonder if it scares you that you can't store your beauty.

instead, we talk about the fire in our bellies, and i watch our desire for something grander spill from our mouths. *but i only taste grapes on my lips.* these conversations are not the main event — or the grapes or the seashells. nothing is the main event for an early Thursday afternoon because an early Thursday afternoon was always promised, and that made it too regular to remember.

i know one day, i'll wish i had collected more seashells. i'll wish i had stored these little afternoons when life tasted of grapes and when beauty was as common as possibility. i'll wish i had savored the bittersweet epoch when the sun promised to rise tomorrow, when the light promised to reach us forever.

sweet one

it was an unmemorable day
during a forgettable hour,
but i remembered to say:

it's time to get up now.
open the window and let the light in.

risk and remember to breathe.

friendship

to have friendship is to speak
black opium into a void only entered by you and them.
to see the epic ebb of life,
and hold their brittle hand as they shatter into pieces —

then show them how they look put back together.

because only a friend knows our house of mirrors
and holds up the best mirror.

only a friend
would understand you when you say,

i fear the fear
all around me
and there are bags under my eyes, can you see them?

only a friend would tell you,

who cares? i love you anyway.

because to have a friend

is to love and love

                    and love

until you both fall into the void you've created,

and not alone.

Tokyo

this is your treasure box   it's purple! like the color
between two instruments that shouldn't pair together
but they could   they do   think a trumpet and the drums
you see the city and you think   the city is old and
in many ways new   but you are *new new*   to this city
and to this world   *baby girl in a foreign world*
your hands still shake when you speak   poor baby
but it's okay! because there are rivers and moonlight,
soft sugars and warm tea, rainstorms and train rides,
the Buddhist monk taps on his wristwatch   and the
music that plays sings to us, *youth only lasts once*
you rescind that the grass isn't greener   because it is
you've seen it   you've drank from it and stained
your teeth   the shadows here dance at night
there is night and it is sweet   silver-toned when the
trains stop   but the narrow streets don't, and your feet
struggle to keep with your mind   you vary off course
but was there ever a course? doesn't matter   you'll
reach some end, someday   but shit that's a thought
for a later time   this is not the end   this is plum wine
and counting coins and laughing so hard
your stomach burns   this is falling asleep on a
bench with your best friend and believing that
moments last a little longer if you close your eyes
this is standing atop a skyscraper staring at
the curvature of Earth with a funny feeling that
the city lights are shining for you

inspiration

soon every battle you fought, every wound inflicted, will make sense. you will not be a sad story, a person to be pitied even if that's what you think you want — what you believe you deserve. you will see that we are living the same story in different forms. that yours, too, will be an inspiration.

the end, no end

fellow feeling, thank you for splitting the cosmos
and creating a grotto for carbon to dance below
with craft beer and spittle, and chant prayers
until our arteries drain. it's been a fun ride
and the ride continues — for how long?
not sure. that's the scary truth, the important one.
i believe the length of you will reach an end, but not
the end. there is infinity over the finite, and you,
dear feeling, are bounded. that is what makes you
so special. that is human existence. so, when our bodies
hit the wall, we'll split again, never reaching an end,
just more light
expanding

Notes & Acknowledgements

"candy days repeating" was first published by Sunstroke Magazine in their September Poetry online issue.

"to the house" was first published by the West Trade Review in their Spring 2021, Volume 12 print edition.

"Florida fever dream" references Vincent van Gogh's *The Starry Night*.

"lightning" was inspired by William Shakespeare's "Sonnet 18" and is a nod to the line, "Shall I compare thee to a summer's day?"

Thank you to everyone who has bought this book. It means more than you could ever know. Words have inspired me all my life, and storytelling has shaped who I am. Being able to share my own is a dream come true. I am forever grateful to every reader.

The biggest thanks to my mom for encouraging me to follow every one of my dreams (even the ludicrous ones). There is never a moment that you doubt me. My heart is full of light because of you. You are the reason I never give up. You are why I am able to step into the unknown, and with hope. I love you.

Thank you to Kiana for your endless generosity and friendship. You inspire me every day. I wouldn't be where I am today without you. I wouldn't have the experience needed to write this collection without you. You remind me to take a step back, breathe, and believe — but, most importantly, have fun.

Thank you to Victor for all your creative advice and for always having faith in my work. You warned me it would be tough, but you never questioned if I could do it. I am so grateful to have you as a part of my family.

Warmest thanks to Sarah and Richard for adopting all my weirdness and reminding me to be brave. I'm able to express myself so honestly because of you both.

I'm so appreciative of all my friends and family. Thank you for reading everything I've ever shared. I have so much love for every one of you.

This is Anastasiya Sukhenko's debut poetry collection. Sukhenko is also the author of the short story "The Graveyard Library." Originally born in Kremenchuk, Ukraine, she has spent most of her life living in Florida. She currently resides in California.

You can find her at @anasukhenko on Instagram.

www.ingramcontent.com/pod-product-compliance
Ingram Content Group UK Ltd.
Pitfield, Milton Keynes, MK11 3LW, UK
UKHW021835270726
14058UKWH00002B/173

9 798218 064020